The Curious Observer's Guide to

SLIME MOLDS

OF UC SANTA CRUZ AND BEYOND

Written and photographed by

CARRIE NIBLETT

Edited by

ALEX JONES

The Curious Observer's Guide to Slime Molds of UC Santa Cruz and Beyond
by Carrie Niblett

ISBN 1725169428

Edited by Alex Jones

Published by UCSC Natural Reserves as a resource for students and community
members of University of California, Santa Cruz

Contents

Acknowledgements

I would like to thank the David and Lucile Packard Foundation, whose donation to the Kenneth S. Norris Center for Natural History made it possible for me to recieve funding for this project. Receipt of a Norris Center Studen Project Award enabled this book's initial printing run, but mostly went towards tiny little boxes to hold my slime mold collection. I would also like to thank everyone, past, present and future, who studies slime molds. Your hard work inspires me.

There are so many incredible people who made this project possible. I would like to thank Alex Jones for not only helping edit this project but also for often feeling like a guardian angel to me when I was lost in the slime. Thank you to Chris Lay, Greg Gilbert and Amy Tsang for also helping me edit this project. Dr. Steven Stephenson answered my questions and helped me identify some of my collection. Christian Schwarz helped me with microscopy and measuring spores. Ken Kellman lent me his camera and inspired me with his love and appreciation of the obscure teeny tinies. I would also like to thank the people of the 'Slime Mold Identification and Appreciation' Facebook page for help identifying species and filling my Facebook feed with amazing slime mold photos, information and resources.

I would like to thank all of the naturalists who hang out at the Norris Center-- you inspire me to keep going and to put my whole self into whatever I do. Thank you to my friends and family who listened to me and believed in me even when I didn't.

I would also like to acknowledge the banana slug I stepped on under the Porter bridge while working on this project. I am so very sorry.

Thank you

To Begin With

This project is not my baby. To say that it is my baby would imply that I am its mother. But the slime mold has never needed anything motherly from me. With or without me to stare at it lovingly, snap photos of it growing up and fill journals of my thoughts about it, it persists, often prolifically. I want this book to not only be an informative tool for identifying and understanding how these wild organisms work but also a means to share the beauty, curious nature and my own excitement of slime molds. Roger Tory Peterson likened writing a field guide to a prison sentence, so I wrote a love letter instead. Though it may appear upon first glance like a field guide, this love letter is for my muse, slime mold. Take this 'ode to slime' as your travel companion as you venture into their enigmatic world.

Slime molds can sometimes be tricky to identify in the field and the process of working on this project has helped me (often painfully) learn that it's fine to sometimes leave the ID of a species a mystery. Even without plopping a name on it, there is still so much to learn from getting to know a slime mold. I have only been hanging out with them for about two years and it could easily take a lifetime or three of observations to create a comprehensive field guide--hence my hesitation in calling this one. This book does, however, include common and some not-so-common species one could encounter on the UCSC campus, as well as other temperate, terrestrial ecosystems arounds the world.

From one curious observer to another, slime on my friend.

It's Slime Season

Despite the implications of its name, it's not a mold and it's only sometimes slimy. In their slimiest state, they creep through the forest growing in size and consuming food. They move across logs and leaf litter until their blobishness rises into fruiting bodies, which in their diversity can appear like huge colonies of mauve, shag carpeting growing on a damp log, tapioca pudding dripping down a tree or tiny puffs of cotton candy. They are found all over the world, within the depths of the forest, and luckily for the UC Santa Cruz student, steps away from the classroom. The beauty and strange nature of slime molds have captured both curious observers and scientists alike, but they have proven difficult for science to classify because they are so unlike anything else. They have been associated with plants, but unlike plants they lack chlorophyll. They were once classified as fungi because they reproduce with spores, but they consume food in a way different than any fungi. Slime molds move and feed, but aren't animals. They are unlike anything else--brainless lumps, but lumps on a mission. Perhaps a rogue slime mold spore plummeted though space from some distant exoplantary forest, only to land on our absurd planet to begin a long and beautiful life history of slime molds. Until NASA corroborates this alien theory, however, we shall stick with science. Currently they are classified in the Kingdom Protista, in the Phylum Amoebozoa and their own Class Myxogastria. No matter if you choose to call them protists or divine aliens, they are a group of organisms worth getting to know.

The colloquial term 'slime mold' includes three types of organisms: **Dictyostelids**, **Protostelids** and **Myxogastria**. In this book we will only cover Myxogastria, AKA myxomycetes, AKA acellular slime molds, AKA plasmodial slime molds, AKA the slime of oh-so-many names. For consistency's sake we will refer to this group as **myxomycetes**, or simply just slime molds.

What does slime mold look like?

Slime molds can come in all different shapes, sizes and colors. Some, like *Arcyria deunada*, look like tufts of cotton candy with pink fuzzy heads with pink stalks. Some, like *Ceratiomyxa fruticulosa*, look like tiny, white clusters of coral that should belong in the ocean, but it blankets decomposing logs instead of reefs. Many have no stalks at all and cover their substrate in a colorful, lumpy mass. A large number of slime molds also change colors multiple times in their life. The slime mold *Badhamia utricularis* begins as a creeping orange plasmodium, which turns into dangling, orange fruiting bodies that turn a pale, iridescent blue as they mature. Slime molds are incredibly diverse in appearance but all have a plasmodial stage and a fruiting body stage as unifying features.

Above: *Ceratiomyxa fruticulosa* on a log near Chinquapin Road above Crown College.
Below: *Arcyria* sp. in forest next to the Porter Meadow.

Phaneroplasmodium of a *Didymium* sp. in fall 2016.

Plasmodium

A plasmodial stage is characteristic of all slime molds, but not all plasmodia look or behave the same way. All plasmodia are **acellular,** meaning each plasmodium is basically one giant cell. It can have hundreds to billions of nuclei and is bound by a cell membrane.

Sclerotium- If environmental conditions are bad, like being too cold or too dry, the plasmodium can turn into a dormant structure called a sclerotium. Upon the resumption of suitable conditions the sclerotium gives rise to a new plasmodium.

There are three different kinds of named plasmodia. More types of plasmodia exist and act as hybrids of these three kinds, but are little studied and remain unnamed.

Phaneroplasmodium- This plasmodium appears like a fan-shaped network of veins with a thick slime sheath and pulsates while it moves over substrate. The fan shape allows the plasmodium to rapidly increase the surface area it covers, maximizing its food intake. It eventually gives rise to tens to hundreds of fruiting bodies. This kind of plasmodium is the most easily seen in nature as it can be large and brightly colored. Slime molds in the Trichiales and Physarales orders characteristically produce phaneroplasmodia.

Above: *Leocarpus fragilis* plasmodium that I collected in fall 2016 in an attempt to cultivate it. It hardened into a sclerotium by the next day.

Below: Phaneroplasmodium of *Badhamia utricularis* found in winter 2017.

Aphanoplasmodium- This inconspicuous plasmodium is rarely seen in nature. It looks like fine, thin, black or unpigmented networks of veins that sometimes gain pigment with maturity. This kind of plasmodium does not turn into a sclerotium when conditions are poor, but instead hardens into droplets that can quickly reform into plasmodium when favorable conditions return. This kind of plasmodium is common in the Stemonitales order.

Protoplasmodium- This is the most primitive type of plasmodium. It is microscopic through its entire existence until it gives rise to a single, small fruiting body. It is generally is found on the bark of living trees and has the ability to creep through small cracks and spaces. It has the advantage of being able to produce fruiting bodies quickly when conditions are good. This plasmodium is characteristic of all of the Echinosteliales order and some species of the Liceales order.

Above: Mature aphanoplasmodium of *Stemonitopsis typhina* seen in winter 2017.
Right: Veins of a *Badhamia utricularis* phaneroplasmodium found in winter 2017.

Fruiting Body

The fruiting body rises out of the plasmodium and contains the spores of the slime mold, which are its means of reproduction. The change from plasmodium to fruiting body depends on environmental conditions including light, temperature, moisture and pH.

Spores

The spores are the unit of reproduction, which will get dispersed from the fruiting body, germinate and continue the organism's life cycle. They are visible microscopically and are shaped as imperfect circles. Depending on the species they can be textured in a variety of ways including lightly to heavily warty, covered in small to large spines, reticulate (covered in net-like ridges) or banded, with almost no spores entirely smooth. They are 5-15 micrometers in diameter; for comparison, a micrometer is about 0.00004 inches, a human blood cell is 5 micrometers wide and a human hair is 75 micrometers wide. Spores have been found to be every color except blue or green. Physarales and Stemonitales orders are generally dark spored while the rest are light or brightly colored.

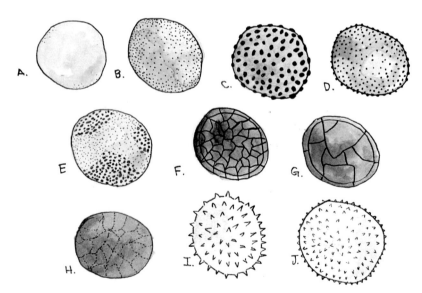

A: Nearly smooth. B: Roughened. C: Heavily warty. D: Lightly warty with a pocket.
E: Warty with more heavily warty clusters. F: Banded and densely reticulate.
G: Banded and reticulate. H: Light or broken reticulate. I: Spiny. J: Lightly spiny.

Comparision of two differently shaped sporangia fruiting bodies.
Left is *Stemonitopsis typhina* with fungi growing on it. Right is a *Hemitrichia* sp.

Fruiting bodies can vary greatly in size, color and quantity among species, but they all serve the same purpose: spreading spores. There are four different kinds of fruiting bodies in slime molds.

Sporangium (plural sporangia)- This is the most common type of fruiting body. They are small, usually around 1-3 mm (very rarely above 15 mm) in height and are usually clustered and uniform. The fruiting bodies can be stalked or sessile (no stalk).

Aethalium (plural aethalia)- This type of fruiting body appears as a dome or imperfect mass on its substrate. Aethalia vary greatly in size, are always sessile and are composed of a mass of fused sporangia.

Pseudoaethalium (plural pseudoaethalia)- These fruiting bodies mimic the dome shape of aethalia, but are made up of many crowded sporangia that are not fused. Most are sessile but can rarely be stalked.

Plasmodiocarp- These fruiting bodies retain the shape of their plasmodial veins and are always sessile. They can be netlike but are most often straight or curved. A common species with this type of fruiting body is *Hemitrichia serpula*.

Left: Sessile *Didymium* sp. Right: Stalked *Didymium* sp.

Above: Aethalium of *Enteridium lycoperdon.*
Below: Crowded sporangia of the pseudoaethalium of *Dictydiaethalium plumbeum.*

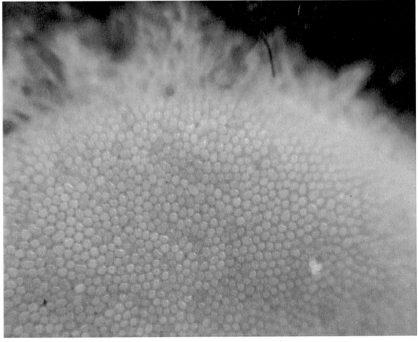

The structural elements of a fruiting body may consist of the following:

1. Sporotheca- This is the head-like part of the sporangium that holds the spores.

2. Capillitium- These are the threadlike elements that are found in the spore mass of some species, but are not connected to the spores themselves. They can form dense nets or have free ends which are called **elaters**. A **pseudocapillitium** is the name of the mass of threads among the spores in some aethalium or pseudoaethalium fruiting bodies. It has characteristics of a true capillitium but its threadlike structures are much more irregularly shaped and it is thought to be formed from leftover material from the plasmodium.

3. Peridium- This is a protective covering that can vary from thick to thin and encloses the spore mass before maturity. Spores are released when the peridium breaks off. The remaining peridium can appear as a cup shape (see calycylus) at the base of the spore mass, can open up like a flower or can completely break off (and the way it breaks off is an important identifying feature). In certain species, the peridium has an iridescent appearance. This is produced by light interference dependent on the thickness and refractive index of the peridium's material.

4. Calyculus- This is the cup-shaped structure at the base of the spore mass. It is the part of the peridium that persists post-maturity in some species.

5. Stalk- The structure that raises the spore mass above its substrate. There can be much variation in its appearance: stalks can be very thin and delicate, short and stout, thick and covered in bumps and veins or anything in between. There can even be variation in stalk length within the same species depending on the environmental conditions present while it was developing. Some species consistently have no stalk at all, while others have been seen as both stalked and sessile.

6. Columella- The structure in some species where the stalk extends into the spore mass. It can be a thickened peridium in sessile fruiting bodies.

7. Hypothallus- This can surround the base of a single fruiting body or be a layer at the base of many fruiting bodies. The plasmodium deposits it when fruiting occurs and it can be thick or thin and transparent or brightly colored depending on the species.

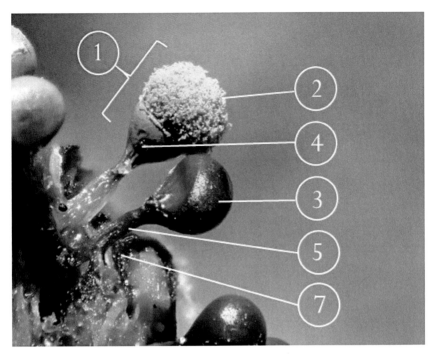

Above: *Trichia decipiens*
Below: Young *Stemonitis* sp.

Part 2: Life Cycle

Chicken or the egg question aside, let us begin. First, a spore is released from a fruiting body. Under proper conditions, many of which are still unknown, the spore germinates and makes 1-4 **haploid** unwalled cells. If free water is present when the cells are released generally they will be **flagellated**, meaning they will have a small whip-like tail which makes them mobile. These flagellated cells are called **swarm cells**. If no free water is available, the protoplast cells released instead are **amoeboid** cells, called **myxamoebae**, which have no flagellae. Swarm cells and myxamoebae serve the same function, which is to ingest food and grow, and are therefore sometimes both called **ameboflagellae**.

Next the ameboflagellate cells divide in half through a kind of asexual reproduction called **binary fission**. If conditions become unfavorable (e.g. too dry or lacking in food) during this time, an ameboflagella can harden into a dormant structure called a microcyst. A microcyst is formed when the **protoplast** of the ameboflagella conglomerates to make a thin protective cell wall around itself. When conditions become favorable again it can reverse back into an ameboflagellate cell and carry on.

After a critical number of ameboflagellate cells are formed, sexual reproduction occurs and two compatible swarm and/or myxomoebae cells fuse to form a **diploid zygote**. In this process the protoplasms of the two cells fuse to become a zygote. The zygote feeds though a process called **phagocytosis**, which is described in more detail below, and grows through numerous mitotic divisions. The zygote will grow bigger and bigger though mitosis and will eventually become the **plasmodium**. The plasmodium remains **acellular,** meaning it is one giant cell that can contain several hundred to billions of nuclei.

If conditions are poor the plasmodium can form into a dormant, hard sclerotium made of masses of **macrocysts**, which themselves are masses of smaller multinucleated cells. When or if favorable conditions resume, the macrocysts give rise to a new plasmodium and the life cycle will resume. The sclerotium can remain viable for several years while waiting for proper environmental conditions.

Depletion of food source and/or changes in the temperature, moisture or pH can trigger a mature plasmodium to begin the next stage of the life cycle, where a single to many fruiting bodies will arise. As fruiting bodies begin to form, the plasmodium becomes thicker and forms the **hypothallus,** which in some species can appear as a thick sheet between the substrate and bottom of the stalk on a fruiting body. During this time the plasmodium will rise up in bumps that will each continue to rise and contract at the base to form the stalk and expand at the top to form the head of a **sporangium**. One plasmodium can produce a single or hundreds of fruiting bodies. Spores form as cell walls develop around the diploid nuclei. The spores will eventually mature, germinate and the cycle continues. During this time the capillitium is formed, which is the thread-like interior of the sporangium. It rises from the coalescence of small cavities containing different materials from the protoplasm.

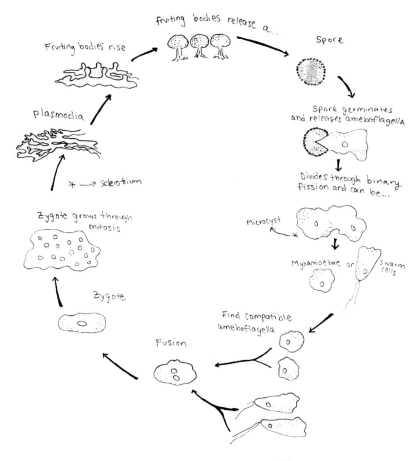

Life cycle of a slime mold

Part 3: How and where can I find
slime molds?

Where is slime mold?

I have always thought that the most amazing part of our campus is how immersed one is in nature. You really have no choice but to witness the wonders of the natural world whether you're eating in a dining hall, walking to lecture or running the track at the East Field. Finding a slime mold is a kind of treasure hunt. If you have or develop an eye for the teeny-tinies of this world, know what kind of environment slime molds like and pay attention to some other clues and cues like the weather and substrate, then finding slime molds is no different than finding the wildflowers in Porter Meadow or our friend Hank the turkey--it's just on a much smaller scale. On our campus, these charming organisms are right under our slimy mustaches. One of the most prolific fruitings of *Lycogala epidendrum* I've seen was steps away from Baskin Engineering. I saw a stunning colony of *Arcyria denudata* right next to the Kresge bridge. The only places I've seen *Leocarpus fragilis* on campus were in the leaf litter next to a dumpster at College 10 and next to a different dumpster at Oakes. Although it may not be the best decision you've ever made, you could probably check next to every dumpster on campus and find at least one slime mold.

Dumpster ecology aside, on our campus you are most likely to find slime molds on damp, decomposing logs and stumps. I see them most often on oaks, especially tanoaks, occasionally madrones and California bay, but rarely on redwoods or manzanitas. Most prefer soft, decomposing wood but some like *Ceratiomyxa fruticulosa* and *Lycogala epidendrum* seem to also like the hard, outer bark layer of fallen logs. You are also likely to find them in leaf litter; I have found several species growing on redwood needles and fallen bay leaves. Slime molds can also be **corticolous** (residing on live vegetation), but this is much less commonly seen both in general and on our campus. Worldwide there are also 114 species known to occupy the tantalizing substrate of both domestic and wild animal dung. So maybe check out some of the cow paddies in the Mima Meadow--you could see some cool shit.

One of the best tips I can give for slime mold hunting (and maybe life in general, though nobody asked) is that you won't know until you go. Most of us probably have an inner pessimist that needs to be shushed. I always try to push back and challenge that little voice that tells me 'you won't see anything over there, so don't bother.' Defy your biases and check those areas where you can't imagine slime molds existing. Even if you don't find any, if you look long enough I bet you'll see some incredible insects, fungi, bryophytes, lichen or so many other fascinating organisms.

Above: Corticolous *Physarum* sp. enjoying it's grassy substrate in the Great Meadow in spring 2017. Below: *Physarum* sp. loving it's damp, decomposing log substrate in fall 2016 within Upper Moore Creek, east of Porter and Kresge.

One of the things I love about slime molds is that you can find them throughout the entire year. Fall and spring are the best times to look because we get enough rain during these seasons to keep substrates wet, but not too much to wash the slime molds away. But even in the hottest parts of summer I have been able to find large fruitings of *Fuligo septica, Hemitrichia* sp. and *Comatricha* sp.

How can I see them?

Since most slime mold fruiting bodies are less than 3mm tall, a hand lens is an incredible tool for seeing their details. Finding them in the first place, however, can be the tricky part. Patience and attention to detail are required to spot these tiny beings and you'll find that it becomes easier with practice. The more time you spend searching for slime molds and looking at slime molds, the higher the likelihood that you might notice them looking right back at you!

How can I photograph them?

My slime mold photography career started with a clip-on camera phone macro lens. I cannot recommend these highly enough. With these it is possible to get some truly incredible shots without having to spend more than $12. For the purpose of this book I mainly used a Canon DSLR with a 100mm macro lens. I also occasionally used a Canon or Olympus point-and-shoot camera, and a photo or two that are included were taken with a cell phone and the clip-on macro lens. A tripod can also be a valuable tool, especially when using a DSLR, but I have found that using my backpack or sweatshirt to position the camera at different angles works almost just as well and it's nice not having to carry extra equipment. I have also found that putting the camera on a self-timer setting allows me to get the clearest shots. Setting a 2 second delay prevents the movement of my hands pressing the shutter release button from shaking the camera. Another photography tip is to try to get down on the same level as the slime mold, and imagine you are a tiny little springtail looking up at it. I have found that photos from this angle are more aesthetically pleasing and include many more important details, such as what the stalk looks like, compared with taking photos from above.

For the microscopy photos taken in this book, I mounted a small piece of the fruiting body on a slide with 70% ethanol and a 3% KOH solution. Most photos were taken at 40x using a compound microscope connected to a camera and computer and taken with image capture software. Some microscopy photos taken at different focal depths have been merged in Adobe Photoshop to show the most possible detail.

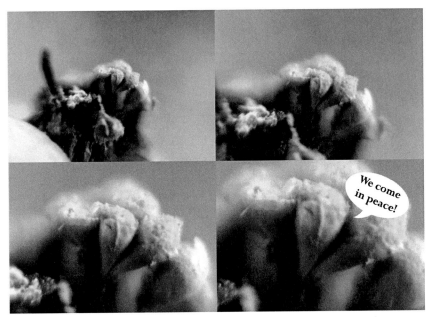

A stare down with *Hemitrichia* sp. You may experience this too once your brain has gone to slime.

Arcyria denudata captured with a macro clip and a HTC cellphone. Not so crummy if I do say so myself.

Part 4: Behavior and Lifestyle

What and how they eat

Slime molds eat only during the plasmodial stage. The primary food source for slime molds is bacteria, but they also feed on algal cells, yeast and the **hyphae**, spores and fruiting bodies of fungi. The plasmodium is capable of absorbing food directly from the environment by engulfing the food in a process called **phagocytosis**. During this process the food particles become surrounded by temporary protrusions on the surface of the **ameboflagellae** that are called **pseudopodia**. The food particles then become surrounded by a membrane, called a food vacuole, which secretes enzymes to digest the food.

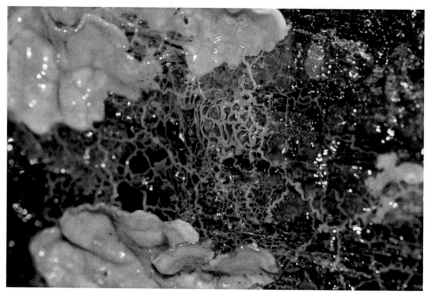

Badhamia utricularis plasmodium munching on *Stereum* sp. fungi in winter 2017.

Locomotion

Physical movement happens during the plasmodial stage. A slime molds moves, looking for nutrients until it has exhausted its food sources. It moves very slowly, at around 2 mm an hour, but it's slime on a mission! The process that propels movement is called **cytoplasmic streaming**, or just streaming. Streaming is necessary for locomotion, but can also occur in stationary plasmodia. The force behind streaming is an ATP fueled actin-myosin contractile system of fibers. Essentially these work similarly to our muscles but on a very small scale. Actin-myosin are units that form fibers, like our muscle tendons, that are contracted by ATP, a molecule that stores and supplies a cell with energy. The contraction of these fibers forms a hydraulic pressure that fuels the forward motion. Streaming can be visible under a microscope or with time lapse photography, appearing like a rhythmic pulsation as the fibers contract. The outermost end of the plasmodium will bulge and pulsate in a forward direction followed by a pulsation in the reverse direction--sort of a two steps forward, one step back motion.

The same *Badhamia utricularis* as shown to the left, about one week later.

Dirty Tricks (Adaptations)

Along with the formation of microcysts and a sclerotium when environmental conditions become too harsh, slime molds have evolved some other tricks in order to remain competitive. One of these tricks is to reduce the amount of time it takes for a plasmodium to create mature spore-producing bodies. **Corticolous** slime molds have perfected this strategy. These slime molds live on the bark or leaves of live plants and are less commonly seen on our campus. Because these microhabitats have fewer accessible nutrients or bacteria for consumption than decaying material, there is more competition amongst live bark or leaf-dwelling organisms for resources. To deal with this issue, corticolous slime molds will sporulate quickly--within only 2-4 days after germination. In contrast, most slime molds seen around campus dwell on decaying vegetation or bark, where there are abundant bacteria and nutrients available for them. Because of this abundance of food they have much slower sporulation, spending more time as a plasmodium and taking a longer time to create mature spore-producing fruiting bodies.

Having a head and stalk provides another evolutionary advantage, as they elevate the fruiting body above its substrate and allow for better spore dispersal than being sessile. Around 70% of slime molds are stalked, most likely for this reason. Another spore dispersal tactic is having round, ornamented spores that are ~8 to 12 micrometers in size. Almost no slime mold spores are perfectly smooth, suggesting that evolutionarily these characteristics allow for the best long-range air dispersal.

Above: Corticolous *Physarum* sp. on a California bay leaf.
Right: A product of coincidence rather than corticolousness, *Physarum globuliferum* perches on top of a small mushroom.

Part 5: Ecology

Insects

Many arthropods benefit from eating or nesting inside of slime molds. It is common to see springtails (Collembola) and various beetles feeding on plasmodia and fruiting bodies. Insects burrow into fruiting bodies and eat the protein-rich spores, but then also inadvertently spread the spores, helping the slime mold disperse. There are very small beetles, appropriately referred to as slime mold beetles, which appear to be slime mold specialists and feed on plasmodia and fruiting bodies.

There are also a few species of flies that breed exclusively in slime molds. They lay eggs and build a web-like covering around the puparium (where the larvae and pupae will develop) on a plasmodium. The larvae can feed on the plasmodium once they hatch, and as the slime mold and flies both mature the flies will unwittingly spread the spores by carrying them away.

A very webby *Hemitrichia* sp. in winter 2017 behind Colleges 9 and 10.

Fungi

Some fungi eat slime molds, and some slime molds eat fungi. *Badhamia utricularis* is an exceptionally fungus-loving slime mold. I have seen its plasmodia creeping around *Stereum* sp. fungi and crust fungi. Some ascomycete fungi (Phylum Ascomycota) grow on slime molds. Some are even known to grow exclusively on myxomycetes. These fungi are very small and cover the surface of the slime mold's fruiting body. They give the fruiting body the appearance of looking moldy…moldy slime.

Above: *Badhamia utricularis* dangling from a *Stereum* fungus, which is also growing a mold (so many levels!).

Below: Ascomycete fungi on a *Trichia* sp.

Bryophytes

Two species, the rare *Barbeyella minutissima* and more common *Lepidoderma tigrinum,* associate with leafy liverworts as substrate. Other bryophyte interaction is thought to be coincidental due to both organisms preferring the same environments.

Humans

The most common relationship between humans and slime molds is one of mutual ignorance. However, some people have chosen to get to know the slime molds by poking around damp logs and leaf litter, reading books or talking about this crazy organism. If you so choose, you can study it and marvel at it, which is fun! And you can also apparently eat certain species. Which also seems fun! Indigenous people of Mexico supposedly collected, fried and ate the plasmodia of young *Fuligio septica* and *Enteridium lycoperdon* like scrambled eggs. If you choose to try this out, please send me an email about it. I am endlessly curious but my timing has never been right in finding either of these species in their plasmodial stages.

I have never seen a slime mold/bryophyte interaction on campus, so I can only assume that this is exactly how it goes down.

Part 6: Taxonomy

Taxonomy

Slime molds have been part of a taxonomical tug-of-war since they were first described in the mid-1800s. In 1829 the Swedish mycologist Elias Magnus Fries described many species of slime mold and classified them among fungi in the now scientifically obsolete class Gasteromycetes, which contained fungi including puffballs, earthstars and stinkhorns. Fries described them in their own suborder called Myxogasteres. In 1833 the German botanist Heinrich Link substituted the name given by Fries with the name Myxomycetes from the Greek words *myxa*, meaning slime, and *myketes*, meaning fungi, and also associated them with fungi. In 1859 the German botanist, microbiologist and mycologist Anton de Bary argued it was a lower form of animal life and coined the term Mycetozoa, meaning fungous animals. Later de Bary classified it as a microorganism but did not know what kingdom it belonged to. They were more recently classified as fungi by C. W. Martin and C. J. Alexopoulos in 1949 because they reproduce with spores. However that classification did not fit because they ingest food by taking it into their bodies to break it down, unlike fungi which release an enzyme to digest food externally. The fungi classification also does not fit because it was found that slime mold spores produce ameboflagella that form the locomotive plasmodium, unlike fungi whose spores produce mycelium.

Today they are classified based on molecular and evolutionary systematics instead of by their physical traits. Slime molds are currently classified in the Kingdom Protozoa, Phylum Amoebozoa and Class Myxogastria. Since the term 'slime mold' refers to three different kinds of organisms, the term Myxomycetes is commonly used although it is no longer formally taxonomically correct. It is also still generally studied in the realm of mycology despite not being a fungus. Alas.

Other Slimes to Befriend

Dictyostelids, protostelids and myxogastria are the three different organisms called slime mold, all of which are part of the Eumycetozoa class of amoeboid protozoa and possess spore-producing fruiting bodies during a part of their life cycle. Dictyostelids and protostelids are single-celled, inhabit soil and consume bacteria. Unlike myxomycetes, whose locomotive stage involves a fused plasmodium, these two groups instead have individual cells coming together (but not fusing) to form what is called a 'slug,' which requires cooperation from the individual cells as they work as an organized community. They live most abundantly in the duff and topsoil but you need a compound microscope to see them. Dictyostelids are an incredible example of biological altruism; instead of themselves turning into fruiting bodies, many cells sacrifice themselves to make the stalk of a fruiting body and therefore never get to reproduce. Protostelids are the morphologically simplest members of the Eumycetozoa class, and while similar in size and single-cellularity to dictyostelids, they are structurally more similar to myxogastria but produce only a single spore.

Part 7: Is this slime mold?
(Short answer: no)

During my time spent slime mold hunting, I've seen a lot of things that may appear to be slime molds at first glance, but are something else entirely. Here are some descriptions of some of the fascinating non-slime mold things that you may encounter.

Fungi & True Mold

Some fungi have peculiar tube or club-like shapes that can look like slime molds. *Calocera cornea* and *Xylaria hypoxylon* are two small, club shaped fungi that grow directly out of woody substrate. One way to tell these apart from a slime mold is that they are much hardier and thicker than stalked slime molds. When young, these fungi can be of similar size to a stalked slime mold but lack the characteristic bulbous head.

Different crust fungi found on our campus can also appear to look like the plasmodial stage of a slime mold. One major difference is the texture, however, as crust fungi can be fuzzy or velvety and will rarely appear to have the sliminess of a plasmodial slime mold.

One fungal group that does mimic the sliminess of plasmodia is jelly fungi. Jelly fungi often grow out of logs and I have seen jelly fungi that are yellow, orange, black, white and brown on campus. Jelly fungi typically have a much higher volume and many more folds than plasmodial slime molds, which generally lay flat over their substrates.

Cup fungi are another group that can be confused with slime molds. Cup fungi belong to the Ascomycota phylum of fungi and certain species like *Bisporella* sp. that are small in size can resemble slime molds and occupy similar substrates. They can be told apart by their smooth, cup or disk-shaped surfaces, each often connected to its substrate by a thick, short stalk.

While I'm sure most of us know what mold growing on an old piece of bread looks like, it can be more difficult to identify out of the context of the kitchen. On our campus it's common to see mold growing out of poop, animal remains or on the pieces of smashed pumpkin that reliably show up after Halloween each year. True molds have a much fuzzier appearance than slime molds and are generally much finer and more tightly packed than slime mold fruiting bodies. They are also usually confined to a white, brown, black or green color palette.

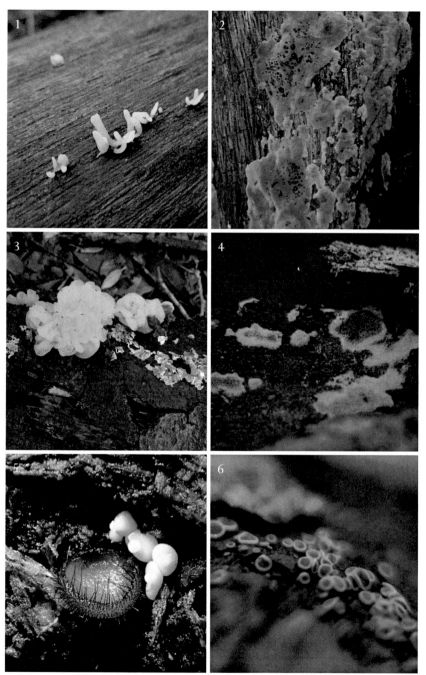

1. Fungi *Calocera cornea*. 2. Purple crust fungi. 3. Jelly fungi, *Tremella* sp. 4. Crust fungi. 5. Cup fungus, *Scutellinia scutellata*, with a young slime mold above it. 6. Ascomycete fungi.

True mold covering an unknown animal poo.

Poo-Poo

A splat of white bird poo on a log or in the duff always seems to catch me off guard. After a harder look it's generally evident that what I am looking at is not slime mold in any way. One of the biggest giveaways is that it's usually a marbled white, black and sometimes purple color, which would be very uncharacteristic of a slime mold plasmodium.

Frass, or insect poo, can also look suspiciously like slime molds. I often see frass in the same cracks and crevasses of decomposing logs as I would expect to find slime molds. I see termite frass most often, which looks like clusters of small, woody, beige colored elongated pill shapes and can have the appearance of very old slime mold fruiting bodies.

Above: Beautiful bird caca.
Below: Termite frass.

Part 8: Species Descriptions

Below are descriptions of the six myxomycete orders as well as descriptions of some species I have identified on campus while working on this project. Those with established common names have these names included in parentheses; common names annotated with my initials (cn) indicate that I made these names up, because somebody has to!

Order Ceratiomyxales

Members of this order produce spores externally, unlike any other order of slime mold. Spores are born on threadlike stalks on the surface of simple or branched columns that rise from the hypothallus. This order contains one family, one genus and four species.

Order Echinosteliales

Members of this order are often too small to be seen in the field. It is highly likely that members of this order are present on the UCSC campus, but I have not collected or described any. All members form sporangia and have a delicate peridium. To the naked eye spores are generally lighter colored and nearly colorless by transmitted light. Members form a protoplasmodium that is colorless or pink.

Order Liceales

Members of this order lack a capillitium and a pseudocapillitium is sometimes present. Sporangium, athaelium, pseudoathalium and plasmodiocarp fruiting body types are represented in this order, with sporangia being the most common. Spores can be pale to dark yellow, red-brown or brown (but never purple-brown) to the naked eye.

Order Trichiales

Members of this order form usually brightly colored stalked or sessile sporangia or rarely plasmodiocarps. The capillitium is made of solid or tubular threads that unite into a net or can be free at the base. Spores are white or brightly colored to the naked eye and nearly colorless, yellow or red by transmitted light.

Order Physarales

Members of this order most often form sporangia and rarely plasmodiocarps or aethaelia. This order is characterized by the usual presence of crystal-like or granular lime (calcium carbonate) deposits which can occur in the stalk, peridium and/or capillitium. Capillitia are threads or tube-like filaments that have limy nodes. Lime is usually recognizable but sometimes due to environmental conditions very little lime is produced, making them difficult to identify. Spores are dark to the naked eye, from black to deep purple to purple-brown, and purple-brown to violet by transmitted light.

Order Stemontiales

Members of this order predominantly have stalked sporangia but the other three fruiting body types are also rarely seen. Members have peridia and capillitia that are not calcareous. When lime is present it is almost always only in the hypothallus and at the base of sporangia. The capillitium is most commonly a network of smooth, dark threads attached to the columella at the top. Spores are dark and vary from black, brown or deep violet to the naked eye and are brightly colored by transmitted light.

Arcyria denudata (Cotton Candy Slime)

Order: Trichiales

Plasmodium is white and the very young sporangia that rise from it look like small, viscid white pearls (bottom right image) on their dead wood substrate, eventually rising to be 2-6 mm tall. Sporangia are usually seen in crowded, large, gregarious fruitings and less commonly seen as a few scattered fruiting bodies. Sporotheca are deep pink in color, cylindrical and sometimes taper narrower near the top (and look like cotton candy!). With maturity they are sometimes dull to brick-red or brown in color. They have slender stalks that are 0.5-1.5 mm tall and are the same color as the sporotheca or darker. The peridium persists in mature fruiting bodies as a small, shallow, funnel-shaped calyculus with an attached capitillium.

Spores are 6-8 micrometers in diameter, red to the naked eye and colorless by transmitted light. Spores have a few scattered warts. Capitillium threads are 3-4 micrometers in diameter and marked with cogs or half rings spiraling around the center. These cogs are attached to the inner surface of the calyculus.

Comments: This species is common and has a cosmopolitan distribution. It can be confused with other *Arcyria* species, especially *Arcyria incarnata*, which is less common and can be distinguished by its redder color, longer stalks, shallower calyculus and a capitillium that is easily detached from the calyculus. I have seen large colonies of this species in very high foot traffic areas, like next to the Kresge bridge and by Building J in Kresge.

Arcyria ferruginea

10 Micrometers

Order: Trichiales

Plasmodium is pale pink and after maturation begins the young sporangia look like tightly packed, small, viscid, bright pink spheres (top right image) on their dead wood substrate. With age, the 1-2 mm sporangia turn brick-red or red-brown and then eventually dull orange or deep mustard in color (left image). They are often found in densely packed clusters. The sporangia can be spherical, ovate or pear-shaped and have 0.3-0.8 mm long stalks. Capitillium is loosely attached to the stalk and is easily detached completely, leaving behind only the large, broad calyculus.

Spores are 9-12 micrometers in diameter, reddish in color to the naked eye and pale yellowish-brown by transmitted light. Spores are lightly warty. Capitillium threads are 5-8 micrometers in diameter and marked with dense transverse bars and warts.

Comments: I found a large fruiting of this species in the Porter Meadow in fall 2016.

Arcyria nutans (cn: Banana Bunch Slime)

Order: Trichiales

A watery white plasmodium gives rise to densely packed, cylindric, stalked or sessile sporangia. Immature sporangia (bottom right image) are 1.5-2 mm tall and at full maturity (left image), once the peridium is shed, can expand to be 4-12 mm tall. Sporangia start out upright but begin to droop with maturity. They are initially bright yellow and begin to dull to a pale buff yellow or ochre color as they mature. The peridium persists as a shallow, textured and translucent yellow calyculus.

Spores are 7-8 micrometers in diameter with an ochre color to the naked eye and nearly colorless under transmitted light. They have a few scattered warts. Capitillium threads are 3-4 micrometers in diameter and marked with spines, rings or other irregular net-like lines.

Comments: Synonymous name, *Arcyria obvelata*. Cosmopolitan distribution. On campus, I saw small fruitings of this species in fall 2016 in clusters smaller than 6 mm in width.

Badhamia utricularis (Hanging Slime Mold)

10 Micrometers

Order: Physarales

Plasmodium is bright orange to yellow on dead wood and is often seen in association with the fruiting bodies of wood-decaying fungi. The plasmodium gives rise to usually large, sometimes over 30 cm long, colonies of stalked and rarely sessile sporangia that often hang and dangle off their substrate. The sporotheca can be oval, spherical or pear-shaped and are 0.5-1 mm in diameter. Young sporangia begin bright orange (top right image) and mature to grey or pale blue (left image), turning deep blue when wet. The peridium appears to be an iridescent rainbow color in the correct lighting. Stalks are weak, flexible, multi-branched and yellow to reddish-brown in color.

Spores are 10-14 micrometers in diameter, blackish brown to the naked eye and violet brown by transmitted light. Spores are distinctly warty and often aggregated into clumps that easily fall apart.

Comments: Cosmopolitan distribution. On campus I would notice orange plasmodia creeping around crust fungi after large rain events. After coming back 2-3 days later it would be apparent that they were *Badhamia utricularis*. I also noticed the fruiting bodies tended to last much longer than other slime mold species and could easily survive big rains.

Ceratiomyxa fruticulosa (Coral Slime)

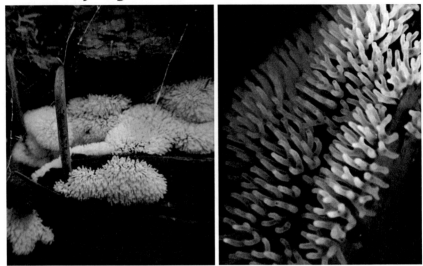

Order: Ceratiomyxales

Plasmodium is white, watery and gives rise to sporangia that consist of a series of clusters of branched or unbranched columns that rise from the hypothallus. The length of columns can vary from 1-10 mm and the quantity of columns can vary from few to many. It is most often slightly translucent and white but can rarely be pale pink, yellow, blue or green as a response to local environmental factors.

Spores are white to the naked eye and nearly translucent by transmitted light. They can be variable in shape and size but most are distinctly oval and are 6-7 micrometers wide x 10-13 micrometers tall.

Comments: This cosmopolitan species is one of the most abundant and distinctive slime molds. On campus I've noticed this species most abundantly around one week after a large rain event and it seems to like soft decomposing wood as well as harder bark as substrate. When conditions dry out quickly following big rain events this species will sometimes dry up, becoming smaller and more opaque. I saw one yellow-orange individual near the Great Meadow; other than that I have only seen white individuals.

Comatricha nigra

10 Micrometers

Order: Stemonitales

Plasmodium is first colorless, then white, and gives rise to scattered or gregarious sporangia. The sporotheca are spherical, oval or slightly pear-shaped. They start out white and viscid before turning pale brown and finally dark brown or black at full maturity. Stalk is black, long, delicate and hair-like and is often 2-6 times the length of the sporotheca, making the total height around 2-8 mm. Peridium does not persist in mature sporangia. The columella reaches into the capitillium, which appears as an intricate net of threads.

Spores are 9-10 micrometers in diameter and lightly warty to almost smooth. They are black to the naked eye and deep violet under transmitted light.

Comments: Cosmopolitan distribution. I've seen this species only a single time on campus, where it was growing upside down on the underside of a log that also had a prolific fruiting of *Badhamia utricularis*.

Cribaria sp.

Order: Liceales

Sporangia are usually stalked and round or pear-shaped. The peridium is often thickened and appears like a net in the lower portion. At maturity most of the sporangium disappears leaving behind the netted portion which looks like a mesh cup that is frequently attached to the base of the calyculus.

Comments: This can be a difficult genus to identify to species. Many distinguishing characteristics can be inconsistent and vary greatly with maturity.

Dictydiaethalium plumbeum

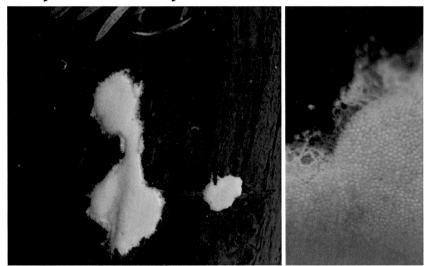

Order: Liceales

Plasmodium is bright pink and found on dead wood and rises into a
pseudoaethalium composed of 1-3 mm tall closely compacted, but not fused,
sporangia. The sporangia sit like fence posts on a thick, persistent, white or silvery
hypothallus that often exceeds the margin of sporangia. When young, sporangia
are bright to orangey pink and at full maturity this species can be dull yellow,
brown, dark olive-brown or less often, dark brick red. Peridium does not persist
in mature fruiting bodies except as thread-like strands on the tips and sides of
individual sporangia.

Spores are olive-brown to clay colored to the naked eye and pale yellow by
transmitted light. They are slightly roughened and 9-12 micrometers in diameter.

Comments: Cosmopolitan distribution. I saw this species on campus several times
in the winter of 2015-2016 growing on the bark of a log in Upper Campus north
of College 9/10.

Enteridium lycoperdon (False Puffball)

Order: Liceales

Aethalium appears as a swollen, perfectly round, imperfect or lumpy half circle against its dead wood substrate. The fruiting body can be 2-8 cm broad and starts out silvery, turning white and then brown. Hypothallus is white and forms a visible margin around the base of the fruiting body. With age, the aethalium ends in a mass of rusty brown spores and pseudocapitial threads (bottom right image).

Spores are rusty brown to the naked eye and pale brown by transmitted light, round or slightly bell-shaped, reticulate over two thirds of the surface and 8-9 micrometers in diameter.

Comments: Synonymous name, *Reticularia lycoperdon*. Cosmopolitan distribution. On campus I've seen this species several times on snags or logs which were not yet very decomposed. Its comparatively large size and white color make it an easy one to spot, but it is often mistaken for a puffball fungus. This species was my gateway slime mold. It was the first I ever noticed and I mistook it for a fungus. I was able to figure out what it actually was through some internet searches and fell down a beautiful slime mold hole that I have yet to climb out of.

Fuligio septica (Dog Vomit Slime Mold)

Order: Physarales

Aethalium appears swollen and can be seen colored white, pale to bright pink, red or pale to bright yellow. Aethalium is usually 2-20 cm wide and 1-3 cm thick. Capitillium can be white, yellow or reddish and is made of a network of interwoven threads. Cortex is sometimes present and can be hard and thick but fragile and separable. Hypothallus is sometimes visible and white. Substrate can be dead or rotting wood, leaf litter, living plants and soil.

Spores are dull black to the naked eye and violet-brown by transmitted light. They are minutely spinulose but mostly smooth and 6-9 micrometers in diameter.

Comments: This is one of the most common and widespread slime molds and it can vary greatly in appearance. It can have a lot of variation in its size and color but can be distinguished from other *Fuligio* sp. by having spores smaller than 10 micrometers. *Fuligo cinerea* usually has a white cortex and *Fuligo intermedia* usually has a thin pale yellow or pale grey-brown cortex. On campus I noticed this species mostly in the summer months. It is also a slime mold you are likely to encounter in more urban areas, especially in gardens and yards.

Leocarpus fragilis (Insect Egg Slime)

10 Micrometers

Order: Physarales

The plasmodium is bright yellow (far left in left image) and gives rise to sporangia that are stalked or nearly sessile on forest litter, wood debris or occasionally corticolous substrate. Sporangia are clustered and shaped as ovals or short cylinders. Sporangia are pale yellow or orange (bottom right image) and turn chestnut brown or dark maroon with maturity (far right in left image). They are 2-4 mm tall, with a peridium that is smooth, shiny, brittle and that consists of three layers. Two types of capillitium are present: one is a rigid network of white branches and the second is a network of colorless flat tubes. The stalks are weak, flat and usually pale brown or yellow and act as an extension of the hypothallus.

Spores are 12-14 micrometers in diameter and coarsely warted. They are black to the naked eye and brown by transmitted light, with one side paler than the other.

Comments: Distribution is limited to temperate and cool temperate regions. This species is most likely found in coniferous forests. On campus I have found it under pine trees on the edge of the Porter Meadow and by dumpsters growing on leaf litter by College 10 and Oakes, all in fall 2016. I also found it next to the dumpster at my house in downtown Santa Cruz a week or two after bringing home a sample from campus.

Lycogala epidendrum (Wolf's Milk)

Order: Liceales

Shaped as perfect or imperfect circles, aethalia are solitary or gregarious and can be scattered or crowded on their dead wood or bark substrate. When immature, they are bright pink and contain a liquidy, bright orange-pink substance inside (that can be popped like a zit!; upper right image). With maturity they turn a grey-brown color and the liquidy insides mature to powdery grey spores (bottom right image). Cortex is thin and has roughened scale-like warts. Pseudocapillitium is composed of long, flat, branching tubes.

Spores are 6-8 micrometers in diameter and marked with reticulate veins. They are pale ochre to the naked eye and nearly colorless by transmitted light.

Comments: This is a widely distributed, easily recognized and cosmopolitan species. If you are one of those people who find joy in popping things (you know who you are) and you want to feel the strange satisfaction of popping these, please just don't pop all the individuals in a group! Leave some to spread their spores. On campus I noticed a prolific fruiting of this species growing on the bark of logs in Upper Moore Creek under the Porter bridge in fall 2016.

Metatrichia floriformis

10 Micrometers

Order: Trichiales

Plasmodium is purple-brown and gives rise to 3-4 mm tall sporangia that are stalked and usually gregarious in large colonies on dead wood. Peridium is shiny and dark blue to black, later breaking into 4-6 petal-like lobes to reveal a mustard yellow to red-orange capillitium. Stalk is slightly veiny and 1-2 mm or more long and reddish brown, turning darker at the top. Hypothallus is dark red.

Spores are 10-12 micrometers in diameter and minutely warty with a smoother, paler pocket in the middle. They are brick-red to the naked eye and pale orange-red under transmitted light. Capitillium threads are 5-6 micrometers in diameter and look like unbranched, rope-like tubes that sometimes coil back on themselves and taper to long points at their ends.

Comments: This is a common and cosmopolitan species. It spread through our campus on dead wood like a weed in the winter of 2017 and would cover logs in large colonies up to nearly half a meter long. I also noticed this species would frequently be covered in a fuzzy white fungus.

Paradiachea caespitosa

10 Micrometers

Order: Stemonitales

White to off-white plasmodium (top right image) gives rise to sporangia that are densely crowded and sessile. Sporangia are dark brown and cylindrical or club shaped and are 1-1.5 mm tall (left image). Peridium is iridescent gold, blue or bronze and tends to be persistent, especially in the lower portion. Hypothallus is delicate, yellow and difficult to see. Capitillium is black and forms a dense network along the entire length of the columella.

Spores are 10-13 micrometers in diameter and black to the naked eye and medium brown under transmitted light. Spores are coarsely warty.

Comments: On campus I found this species on the leaf litter next to the stairs that connect the Porter parking lot to Heller Drive. This species has only been recorded online in five other places in the world (the sixth being our campus, only the second record from the United States!). This may be because it is rare, because of its inconspicuous nature, because there is a lack of people looking or all three.

Physarum nutans (cn: Cookies and Cream Slime)

Order: Physarales

Plasmodium is bright to greenish-yellow and turns watery before fruitification on dead wood or old fungi substrate. Sporangia are stalked and gregarious and 1-1.5 mm tall. Sporotheca are pure white to dull grey in color, round or lenticular shaped and often nodding down. The peridium is coated in lime and breaks off in irregular pieces. Stalks are usually dark in color, fading at the top, slender and wrinkled.

Spores are 8-10 micrometers in diameter, black to the naked eye and pale to lilac brown in transmitted light. Spores are lightly roughened.

Comments: Synonymous name, *Physarum album*. Distribution is cosmopolitan and common. This is a species I have seen in all four seasons on campus. A less common, similar species called *Physarum flavicomum* can be distinguished by its iridescent bronze peridium that is often limeless.

Physarum penetrale

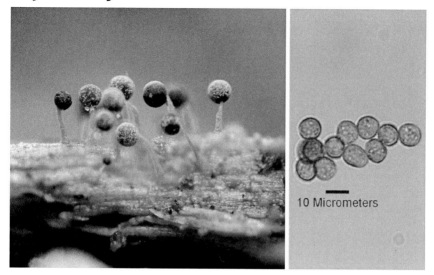

10 Micrometers

Order: Physarales

Plasmodium is orange-yellow and gives rise to immature, yellow club shaped sporangia. Mature sporangia are stalked and 1-2 mm in height. Sporotheca are spherical or oval and can be erect or nodding. The peridium is thin, translucent, greenish-grey to yellowish-green and turns darker as it matures. Sporangia are studded with pale yellow or yellowish-grey scales. Stalk is slender, finely wrinkled, and slightly translucent. It is variable in height and gets slightly wider at the base. Colors can be either a dull red, orange, or orange-brown.

Spores are 6-7 micrometers in diameter, dark brown to the naked eye and lilac brown by transmitted light. Spores are very lightly spiny and spines aggregate into denser patches.

Comments: On campus I saw this species within Upper Moore Creek (the ravine below the Porter and Kresge bridges) in spring 2017 on highly decomposed logs.

Physarum viride

10 Micrometers

Order: Physarales

Plasmodium is yellow to greenish-yellow and gives rise to sporangia on dead wood, old fungi or (less commonly) corticolous substrate. Sporaniga are stalked and gregarious, yellow, greenish yellow, golden or red-orange and 1-1.5 mm in height. Sporotheca are round or lenticular shaped and often nodding down. The peridium is delicate, encrusted in lime and breaks off in irregular pieces above and petal-like lobes below. Stalk can vary from pale yellow, reddish or darker to nearly black.

Spores 7-9 micrometers in diameter, slightly oval and nearly smooth. They are black to the naked eye and violet brown by transmitted light.

Comments: A common and cosmopolitan species. Can easily be confused with *Physarum nutans* but *P. viride* retains its color better. This species can also have a lot of variation in stalk length. On campus I saw this species near the North Remote parking lot in winter 2017.

Stemonitis axifera (Chocolate tube slime)

10 Micrometers

Order: Stemonitales

Plasmodium is white or pale to bright yellow and found on dead wood or leaf litter substrate. Plasmodium gives rise to small or medium sized clustered, erect cylindrical sporangia. Sporangia are 7-15 mm tall and pale to rusty brown. Stalks are black, shiny and 3-7 mm in length.

Spores are bright red-brown to the naked eye and very pale red-brown by transmitted light. They are 5-7 micrometers in diameter and nearly smooth or lightly studded with dots.

Comments: This is a common and cosmopolitan species. *Stemonitis fusca* is also a common species on campus and can be distinguished by its deeper and darker color, slightly taller height and spores that are delicately warty and 8-9 micrometers in diameter. On campus I have noticed these species and other *Stemonitis* spp. during all four seasons. This slime seems to prefer drier weather conditions and easily gets washed away in rain events.

Stemonitopsis typhina

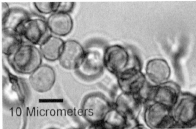

10 Micrometers

Order: Stemonitales

White plasmodium gives rise to gregarious or scattered, stalked sporangia that when immature are translucent white (bottom right image) and when mature are a dark, medium or purple-brown color (left image). Sporangia are 2-5 mm in height and sporotheca are cylindrical or narrowly oval and taper slightly at the top. Peridium is silvery and persists as small patches or sometimes as a shallow calyculus into maturity. The stalk is dark red to nearly black and is often covered with a silvery film at the base. The stalk is generally half the total height of the sporangium, sometimes less. The hypothallus is distinct and reddish brown.

Spores are 6-8 micrometers in diameter, lilac brown to the naked eye and pale lilac brown by transmitted light. They are lightly studded and have scattered dark warts.

Comments: Synonymous name *Comatricha typhoides*. This is a cosmopolitan species and is common, especially on our campus. I have seen this species in all four seasons, sometimes in very large colonies that can be up to 30 cm long. I have also seen it frequently covered in a fuzzy white fungus.

Trichia affinis

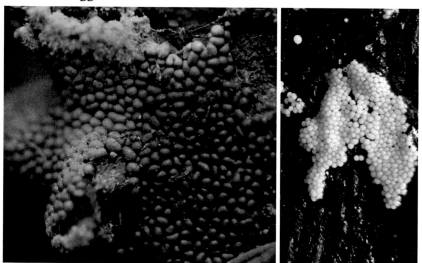

Order: Trichiales

Plasmodium is white and gives rise to sessile, densely crowded sporangia 0.5-0.8 mm in diameter. Sporangia start out white and viscid (right image), then mustard yellow, then mature to red-brown to orange-brown in color with a shining peridium (left image). A yellow-brown hypothallus is sometimes visible.

Spores are yellow to the naked eye and very pale yellow by transmitted light. They are 13-15 micrometers in diameter and banded reticulate. Capitillium threads are 4-6 micrometers in diameter and marked with rope-like, dense reticulations.

Comments: This species looks very similar to other sessile *Trichia* species. In most cases, a view through a microscope is necessary for a species identification. *Trichia scabra* can be distinguished by its smaller spores which are 10-12 micrometers and delicately reticulate and spined capitillial threads. It can also be mistaken for *Trichia persimilis,* which has spores that are warty, marked with broken reticulations and 11-14 micrometers in diameter. On campus these sessile *Trichia* species were extremely prevalent in fall 2016 and I continued to see them throughout the winter and spring of 2017, most abundantly in the forests near Porter Meadow. I have also frequently seen a white stalked fungus growing on this species.

Trichia decipens

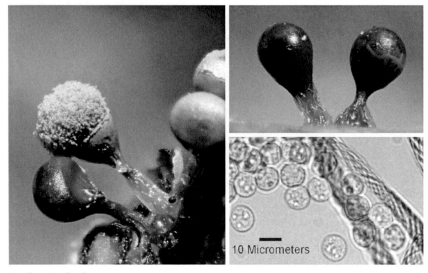

10 Micrometers

Order: Trichiales

White or pale pink plasmodium gives rise to stalked, rarely sessile, gregarious to crowded sporangia. Young sporangia are white to pale pink, then mature to dull yellow, olive-yellow or brown in color. They are 2-3 mm in height at full maturity and inverse cone-shaped. Stalks are up to 1 mm long, dark brown, wrinkled and wider at the base. Peridium is firm and often persists as a deep calyculus.

Spores are olive-yellow to the naked eye and pale yellow by transmitted light. Spores are 10-13 micrometers in diameter and delicately reticulate. Capitillium threads are 5-6 micrometers in diameter, olive-yellow, spirally banded and taper gradually to long slender tips.

Comments: Cosmopolitan distribution. On campus I saw it in winter 2016 and spring 2017.

Trichia varia

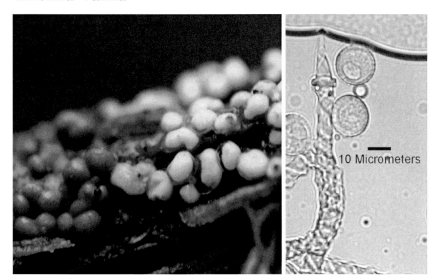

10 Micrometers

Order: Trichiales

Plasmodium is white and gives rise to usually sessile, crowded or well-spaced circular or oval 0.5-0.9 mm broad sporangia. When a stalk is present it is short and black. Immature sporangia are white and viscid and mature to an ochre-yellow or yellow-brown color with a shiny peridium.

Spores are 12-14 micrometers in diameter, yellow to orange-yellow to the naked eye and pale yellow by transmitted light. They are very imperfect circles and delicately warty. Capitillium threads are 3-5 micrometers long, have rope or double helix-like markings and taper to a point on the ends.

Comments: Widely distributed and common in temperate regions around the world. On our campus I saw it much less often than *Trichia perimilis* during the fall and winter of 2016-2017. *Trichia varia* can easily be confused with *T. perimilis* and *Trichia scabra*, both of which usually have much more crowded sporangia and usually visible hypothalli. *T. scabra* also has a more visible, well developed dark hypothallus, smaller spores that are 9-12 micrometers in diameter and capitillium threads that are marked with denser, almost rung-like marks and tips that form a bulb with a short taper.

Glossary

Acellular- Consisting of one cell.

Aethalium (plural aethalia)- A singular fruiting body composed of a mass of fused sporangia that appears as a dome or imperfect mass on its substrate.

Amoeboflagellate- Term used to refer to both swarm cell and myxamoebae life cycle stages.

Aphanoplasmodium (plural aphanoplasmodia)- A type of plasmodium that appears as fine, thin, black or unpigmented veins. Rarely seen due to its inconspicuous nature. Common in the Stemonitales order.

Banded- In the context of describing spores: marked with a line around the perimeter.

Binary fission- The most common kind of asexual reproduction in prokaryotes. The mature parent cell splits in half to produce two new cells.

Calyculus (plural calyculi)- The cup-shaped structure at the base of the spore mass. It is the part of the peridium that persists post-maturity in some species.

Capillitium (plural capillitia)- threadlike elements that are found in the spore mass of some species, but are not connected to the spores themselves.

Columella- Structural part of the fruiting body found in some species where the stalk extends into the spore mass.

Corticolous- Living on live vegetation or bark as substrate.

Cortex- Thick covering of the spore mass in an aethalium or pseudoaethalium.

Cytoplasmic streaming- Process that propels movement and ingests materials and nutrients in the plamsodial stage.

Dictyostelid- One of the three organisms collectively known as slime molds. They are microscopic soil-dwelling amoebae that consume bacteria.

Diploid- Having two sets of chromosomes.

Flagellum (plural flagella)- Long tail-like structure associated with swarm cells and used for locomotion.

Fruiting body- The spore producing organ. Can vary vastly in appearance in slime molds.

Haploid- Having one set of chromosomes.

Hyphae- The branching fibers that make up fungi mycelium.

Hypothallus (plural hypothalli)- The thickened sheet of plasmodium left behind between the fruiting bodies of certain species and their substrate.

Myxamoeba (plural myxamoebae)- Microscopic, uninucleated protoplast that lacks flagella.

Myxogastria- Synonymous term for myxomycete, plasmodial slime mold or acellular slime mold.

Myxomycete- Synonymous term for myxogastria, plasmodial slime mold or acellular slime mold.

Peridium (plural peridia)- Structural part of the fruiting body that is a covering that encloses the spore mass and which breaks off before maturity.

Phagocytosis- The process of ingestion by absorbing food directly through engulfing it and secreting an enzyme to digest it.

Phaneroplasmodium (plural phaneroplasmodia)- Plasmodium that appears as a network of fan shaped veins and gives rise to many fruiting bodies. Common in Trichiales and Physarales orders.

Plasmodiocarp- Type of fruiting body that retains the straight, curve or less often netlike shape of their plasmodial veins and is always sessile.

Plasmodium (plural plasmodia)- Acellular and multinucleated mass of protoplasm that forms the locomotive life cycle stage of slime molds.

Protoplasmodium (plural protoplasmodia)- Primitive type of plasmodium that is invisible to the naked eye and gives rise to a single fruiting body. Characteristic of all of the Echinosteliales order and some species of the Liceales order.

Protoplast- The material comprising the living part of a plant or bacterial cell whose cell wall was removed.

Protostelid- One of the three organisms known as slime molds. It is a soil-dwelling protozoa that consumes bacteria, yeast and spores. Morphologically the simplest type of slime mold and produces only one spore.

Protozoa- Classification for a group of unicellular eukaryotic organisms. All three kinds of slime molds belong to this group.

Pseudoaethalium (plural pseudoaethalia)- A fruiting body type that mimics the dome shape of an aethalium but is made of many crowded sporangia that are not fused.

Pseudocapillitium (plural pseudocapillitia)- A system of tubes, plates or threadlike filaments within the spore mass of some members of the Liceales order that mimics a true capillitium but is formed differently.

Pseudopodium (plural pseudopodia)- A temporary protrusion on the surface of an amoeboid cell used for movement and feeding.

Reticulate- In the context of describing spores: markings that look like a network of many connecting or interlacing branches or lines.

Sclerotium (plural sclerotia)- Hardened, dormant structure that the plasmodium can turn into if environmental conditions are poor.

Sessile- In the context of slime mold fruiting bodies: without a stalk.

Sporangium (plural sporangia)- The most common type of fruiting body. They are generally small, uniform, clustered and can be stalked or sessile.

Spore- The microscopically visible unit of reproduction produced by the fruiting body.

Sporotheca- The head-like part of the sporangium that holds the spores.

Stalk- The structure of a fruiting body that elevates the spore mass from its substrate.

Swarm cells- Microscopic, uninucleated protoplast that has flagella.

Zygote- Diploid cell formed as a result of two fused swarm cells or myxamoeba.

References

Aldrich, H. C. (1982). Influence of Inorganic Ions on Color of Lime in the Myxomycetes. Mycologia, 404-411.

Baldauf, S. L., & Doolittle, W. F. (1997). Origin and Evolution of the Slime Molds (Mycetozoa). Proceedings of the National Academy of Sciences, 94(22), 12007-12012.

Bonner, J. T. (2015). The Evolution of Evolution: Seen through the Eyes of a Slime Mold. BioScience. 65 (12), 1184-1187.

Clark, J., & Haskins, E. F. (2015). Myxomycete Plasmodial Biology: A Review. Mycosphere, 6(6), 643-657.

Clark, J., & Haskins, E. F. (2010). Reproductive Systems in the Myxomycetes: A Review. Mycosphere, 1(4), 337-353.

Dolinko, A., Skigin, D., Inchaussandague, M., & Carmaran, C. (2012). Photonic Simulation Method Applied to the Study of Structural Color in Myxomycetes. Optics Express, 20(14), 15139-15148.

Dörfelt, H., Schmidt, A. R., Ullmann, P., & Wunderlich, J. (2003). The Oldest Fossil Myxogastroid Slime Mould. Mycological research, 107(1), 123-126.

Eliasson, U. (2013). Coprophilous Myxomycetes: Recent Advances and Future Research Directions. Fungal Diversity, 59(1), 85-90.

Everhart, S. E., & Keller, H. W. (2008). Life History Strategies of Corticolous Myxomycetes: The Life Cycle, Plasmodial Types, Fruiting Bodies, and Taxonomic Orders. Fungal Diversity, 29(1), 1-16.

Hoppe, T., & Kutschera, U. (2010). In the Shadow of Darwin: Anton de Bary's Origin of Myxomycetology and a Molecular Phylogeny of the Plasmodial Slime Molds. Theory in Biosciences, 129(1), 15-23.

Keller, H. W., & Everhart, S. E. (2010). Importance of Myxomycetes in Biological Research and Teaching. Fungi, 3(1), 13-27.

Lister, A. (1903). Guide to the British Mycetozoa Exhibited in the Department of Botany, British Museum (Natural History). Order of the Trustees.

Lister, A., & Lister, G. (1911). Monograph of the Mycetozoa.

Martin, G. W., & Alexopoulos, C. J. (1969). The Myxomycetes (Vol. 61). Iowa City: University of Iowa Press.

Rogerson, C. T., & Stephenson, S. L. (1993). Myxomyceticolous fungi. Mycologia, 456-469.

Spiegel, F. W., Lee, S. B., & Rusk, S. A. (1995). Eumycetozoans and Molecular Systematics. Canadian Journal of Botany, 73(S1), 738-746.

Spiegel, F. W., Olive, L. S., & Brown, R. M. (1979). Roles of Actin During Sporocarp Culmination in the Simple Mycetozoan Planoprotostelium aurantium. Proceedings of the National Academy of Sciences, 76(5), 2335-2339.

Stephenson, S. L., & Feest, A. (2012). Ecology of Soil Eumycetozoans. Acta Protozoologica, 2012(3, Special topic issue:" Protists in Soil Processes"), 201-208.

Stephenson, S. L. An Introduction to the Morphology and Taxonomy and of Myxomycetes. Retrieved from slimemold.uark.edu/pdfs/MORPHOTAX.pdf

Stephenson, S. L. (1994). Myxomycetes: A Handbook of Slime Molds. Timber Press (OR).

Stephenson, S. L., & Studlar, S. M. (1985). Myxomycetes Fruiting Upon Bryophytes: Coincidence or Preference?. Journal of Bryology, 13(4), 537-548.

Spatafora, J. Lecture #19 Acrasiomycota: the cellular slime molds. Retrieved from oregonstate.edu/dept/botany/mycology/bot461/class/lecture19.html

Wong, G. Myxomycota. Retrieved from botany.hawaii.edu/faculty/wong/Bot201/Myxomycota/Myxomycota.htm

Bacteria-world.com. How Big is a Micron?

Discoverlife.org

Disjunctnaturalists.com/slime-mould-log

Myxomycetes.net

Index

About the Author

Carrie Niblett graduated with a B.A. in Environmental Studies from UC Santa Cruz in 2017. Her passions for the natural world, teeny tiny things and Easter egg hunts coalesced into a love for slime molds. In the future she hopes to climb more trees and stop having stress dreams about spores.

88730269R00049

Made in the USA
San Bernardino, CA
15 September 2018